Pac

NATURAL

MW01519845

Celebrating the vast mystery of an ocean world, these spectacular color images reveal the richness of the Pacific and the undersea realms encircled by its living necklace of earthquake zones and volcanoes. Called the "Ring of Fire," this embracing circle of life links a fertile chain of ecosystems around the Pacific's shores, from the northern and southern ice caps where seals play, to the warm tropical seas fringing coral islands where translucent goby shimmer through the tentacles of bright anemones. On the reefs, obliging clown fish feed off food caught in the waving fields of leafy cabbage-like corals carpeting the sea bottom. Among the kelp forests, sea lions preen and otters tumble, while garibaldis fiercely defend their territories. The sheepshead and the sea fan bring hot color to this cold water community. Meanwhile, down the Costa Rican coast, spotted moray eels miraculously disguise themselves to escape predators, while Sea of Cortez triggerfish feast on the plankton that seethe above the reef.

Ringed by what makes up the planet's longest and highest mountain range, thrown up by a substratum of volcanic activity, this ancient ocean plays an important part in shaping the character of our weather, the world's climate, and a host of other planetary chemical reactions. It is also truly the crossroads of the history of life on earth. This history began with the sea, in a variety of simple forms: from sponges and jelly-fish, corals and starfish to sea urchins; then to cetaceans (whales and sharks) and primates, including man.

In the past half-century, man has learned more about the ocean than during all of preceding history. The Pacific is the largest of our oceans, covering 71% of the planet, and its intricate web of life still offers a dazzling array of beautiful creatures. However, that richness is now in serious jeopardy because of mankind's activities. With our knowledge should come caring, and these images give cause to hope that we can live in harmony with the natural world. The future of this cradle of life is indeed in our hands.

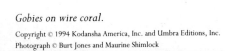

Gobies on wire coral.

Squirrelfish school.

Damselfish over acropora coral.

Sea otters.

Cuttlefish eye.

Emperor angelfish.

Two banded anemone fish.

Sea otter.

Green sea turtle.

Balloonfish.

Lionfish.

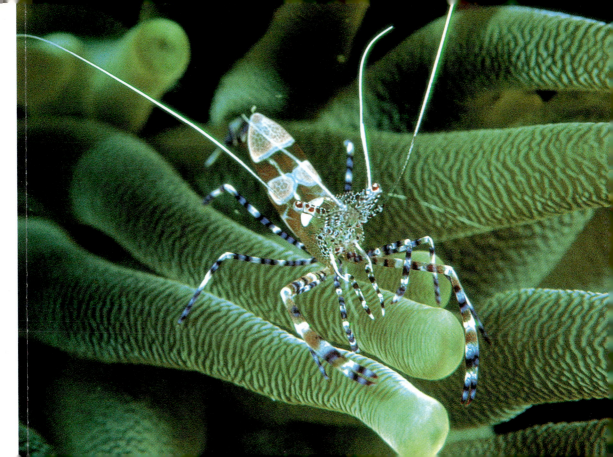

Cleaner shrimp on anemone.

Mixed fish school.

School of poisonous catfish.

White cap anenome fish.

Lyretail coralfish.

Common dolphin.

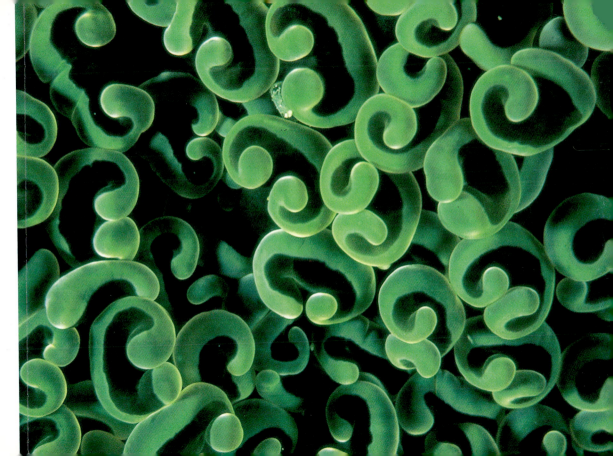

Coral polyps at night.

Anthias.

Starfish.

Coral.

California seal.

Pufferfish.